After

the

Noise

of

Saigon

After
the
Noise
of
Saigon

■ ■ ■ ■ ■ ■

Walter McDonald

■ ■ ■ ■ ■ ■

The

University

of

Massachusetts

Press

Amherst

1988

Copyright © 1988 by Walter McDonald

All rights reserved

Printed in the United States of America

LC 87–20582

ISBN 0–87023–600–8 (cloth); 0–87023–601–6 (paper)

Designed by Barbara Werden

Set in Linoterm Optima

Printed by Cushing-Malloy

and bound by John Dekker & Sons

Library of Congress Cataloging-in-Publication Data

McDonald, Walter.

    After the noise of Saigon/Walter McDonald.

       p. cm.

    ISBN 0–87023–600–8 (alk. paper)   ISBN 0–87023–601–6

    (pbk.: alk. paper)

    I. Title.

    PS3563.A2914A69   1987   87–20582

    811'.54—dc19   CIP

British Library Cataloguing in Publication Data are available

for Carol,

and for Cindy, Kelly, Jacob, and Jordan,

and Chuck

Acknowledgments

Grateful acknowledgment is made for permission to re-
print here poems that appeared earlier in other
publications.

AMERICA: "Night Missions"
THE ANTIGONISH REVIEW (Canada): "Crosswind
    Landings"
THE ANTIOCH REVIEW: "Nearing the End of a Century"
ASCENT: "Between the Moon and Me"
THE BELOIT POETRY JOURNAL: "Rig-Sitting"
CARRYING THE DARKNESS: AMERICAN INDOCHINA—THE
    POETRY OF THE VIETNAM WAR (Avon): "War
    Games"
THE CENTENNIAL REVIEW: "An Object Set in Motion"
    (with another title)
CINCINNATI POETRY REVIEW: "Sundown" (with
    another title)
CUTBANK: "Cousin Billy and the Weather" (with another
    title)
EVENT (Canada): "New Guy"
THE FIDDLEHEAD (Canada): "Bull"
IMAGES: "Praise"
KANSAS QUARTERLY: "Loading a Shotgun"
THE MASSACHUSETTS REVIEW: "In Green Pastures"
MID-AMERICAN REVIEW: "Crashes Real and Imagined"
    and "My Father Quits Another Job"
MISSISSIPPI VALLEY REVIEW: "Jet Flight, the Early
    Years"

THE MISSOURI REVIEW: "Old Men Fishing at
    Brownwood"
NEW ORLEANS REVIEW: "Setting the Torch to Stubble"
OHIO JOURNAL: "The Middle Years" and "With a Wom-
    an Who Looks Like Crystal Gayle"
POET LORE: "After the Noise of Saigon"
POETRY: "When Children Think You Can Do Anything"
PRAIRIE SCHOONER: "Crawling through Caverns" and
    "Reasons for Taking Risks"
THE SEATTLE REVIEW: "Fathers and Sons" and "The
    Night of Rattlesnake Chili"
SENECA REVIEW: "Backpacking the San Juan"
SOUTH DAKOTA REVIEW: "Estacado"
SOUTHERN POETRY REVIEW: "Balance" and "Flood
    Fishing"
SOUTHWEST REVIEW: "Living on Buried Water"
STAND MAGAZINE (England): "The One That Got
    Away"
TAR RIVER POETRY: "Breathe Deeply, and Relax"
TRIQUARTERLY: "The Food Pickers of Saigon"
UNIVERSITY OF WINDSOR REVIEW (Canada): "Nothing
    to Do but Start Over" and "The Eyes in Joe Hall's
    Shed"

Special thanks to Texas Tech University for faculty development leaves and to the National Endowment for the Arts for a fellowship which provided time for writing these poems.

Contents

ONE

Living

on

Buried

Water

When Children Think You
Can Do Anything

Living on hardscrabble, a man is less
than a wolf and knows it, carries a rifle
in season or not. Out here, killing's
always in season, time enough for scruples
sweating in bed with the windows raised.

I hear my kids kicking their sheets.
Like good kids, they blame the heat.
I feel my wife's heat inches away.
They sleep with only me to protect them,
nothing outside I haven't tracked for years,

bobcats and wolves, rattlers that coil
under our trailer like tribal gods.
I'm paid to patch fences around a range
nothing but goats and cows could graze.
I keep the stock tanks full, the buzzards hoping.

When cows stray down arroyos, the wolves
are sure to follow, circling a calf too weak
to waddle. If I can drop one wolf by moonlight,
the others tuck-tail and run. If I'm late,
next morning I drive the cow out

■ ■ ■ ■ ■ ■ ■ ■ ■ ■ ■

wide-eyed and frothing, her full bag swaying,
mesquite and cactus wedging us apart. That night,
I splash my face a long time at the pump
and comb my hair and shave, roll down my sleeves
and go inside as if nothing's happened.

The Food Pickers of Saigon

Rubbish like compost heaps burned every hour
of my days and nights at Tan Son Nhut.
Ragpickers scoured the edges of our junk,
risking the flames, bent over,
searching for food. A ton of tin cans

piled up each month, sharp edged, unlabeled.
Those tiny anonymous people could stick
their hands inside and claw out whatever
remained, scooping it into jars, into their
mouths. No one went hungry. At a distance,

the dump was like a coal mine fire burning
out of control, or Moses' holy bush
which was not consumed. Watching them labor
in the field north of my barracks, trying
to think of something good to write my wife,

I often thought of bears in Yellowstone
our first good summer in a tent. I wrote
about the bears, helping us both focus
on how they waddled to the road and begged,
and came some nights into the campground

■ ■ ■ ■ ■ ■ ■ ■ ■ ■ 5

so long ago and took all food they found.
We sat helplessly naive outside our tent
and watched them, and one night rolled
inside laughing when one great bear
turned and shoulder-swayed his way toward us.

Through the zipped mosquito netting
we watched him watching us. Slack-jawed,
he seemed to grin, to thank us for all
he was about to receive from our table.
We thought how lovely, how much fun

to be this close to danger. No campers
had died in that Disneyland national park
for years. Now, when my children
eat their meat and bread and leave
good broccoli or green beans

on their plates, I call them back
and growl, I can't help it. It's like hearing
my father's voice again. I never tell them
why they have to eat it. I never say
they're like two beautiful children

I found staring at me one night
through the screen of my window,
at Tan Son Nhut, bone-faced. Or that
when I crawled out of my stifling monsoon
dream to feed them, they were gone.

■ ■ ■ ■ ■ ■ ■ ■ ■ ■

Living on Buried Water

This chalk dirt yields sweet onions,
beans, red peppers that make us weep.
Two times a year it rains, run-off
that tumbles stones down arroyos.
Witching with sycamore,
we stalk dry acres for springs
to soak caliche. It never works,
though we've heard rumors.
Flat as a desert, studded with cactus,
hardscrabble farms never need fencing.
Cliffs slough off each year
down canyons. We plant curved rows
and call it home. Our pets are coyotes
that sleep in the sun. The only snakes
are rattlers. Horned owls patrol the night
and stare like dark eyes over us.
We hear the mice they kill. Hawks
glide on thermals shimmering like lakes
in another county. Each time a hawk
plummets and scoops a rabbit like a ladle,
someone takes a stick and goes there,
witching. Sometimes a twig drags down to water
and we risk digging. We haven't found it,
but we believe it's here.

Praise

Under the threat of summer, trees
bring forth their fruit, here in a zone

so dry no trees grow native. The last
late killing frost was years ago.

We're overdue. Thousands of robins
dip down and believe it's spring,

listening to the tongues of sparrows
which seem to sing, bland little birds

that never go anywhere all winter,
and somehow survive.

In Green Pastures

It's grass, not bulls,
spring cattle need.
The clink and creaking of gates
alert them. The man who fed them

silage and grain all winter
is calling. Riding
high on his saddled horse,
he swings the bars of a wide gate

outward, out of the packed
dust and splatter
of the barnyard. Fields fallow
all winter beyond fences are green

at last. Alfalfa opens
before them like
a dream of real pastures.
For weeks they have smelled a vinegar

sweetness in the wind,
and trudged beside
barbed fence wires, restless,
mounting each other's backs, desiring

something other than a bull.
Surprised, at last
they find a feast before them.
It sways like the playa lake

when it's full and blowing
in a storm. Aroused,
almost dizzy, tails swishing, they
stagger through pastures rolling thick

and tender under hooves.
They bury their tongues
deep in green hours they believe
will last forever. Their round eyes glaze,

they never blink, they eat
as if they're waltzing.
They follow the lead of their lips,
and bells around their necks are ringing.

  ■ ■ ■ ■ ■ ■ ■ ■ ■

Setting the Torch to Stubble

To make fire roll we waited for the wind.
From the east a sluggish low blew in,
time to torch the stalks
and burn dead grain fields level.
Flames leaped down rows laid east

to a deep caliche canyon
where our flat world ended. Skunks
and rabbits poured down the canyon
like a spillway. Hawks swooped
through black smoke swirling.

We roamed the rows
and clubbed field mice and rattlers.
We believed in the flames
we heard snake eggs explode.
My mother's daddy grew up knowing

stubble had to burn,
the tight-packed Georgia loam
all his back could break.
Each year, cane blazed so fierce
the hill stones split.

Now, plains fields are loose,
blow-sand even mules could plow,
and we have tractors. Here,
we let grain stubble rot
and plow the mulch for planting.

Our yields increase,
our steel barns overflow. Year-round
hawks glide and sidle.
There are no mice,
and rattlers are everywhere.

The Digs in Escondido Canyon

The clues are here like dominoes
pulverized in sand—a tusk,
the heel bone of a wolf, the spine
of a dinosaur, a few dots of fossils
which must have had a sea. Nothing
about these plains predicts a river
but this dry canyon. Comanches
watered here for years.
Shards of potters centuries ago
wedge up like skulls. Trees grow
from their bones, the only native bark
on plains too dry for roots.
How many nights did people
wandering deserts lie down together,
fearing all evil under the stars,
guarding their firelight from fangs
and others on two feet, sleeping
with blunt tools and spears all night
in this valley of the shadow of water,
dry now, nothing but white caliche
and bones, measured and staked,
each century an inch, each of us kneeling,
troweling and brushing the dust,
praising the slightest sign of life.

Estacado

Great-grandmother in 1880
raised eight children on plains
she called heaven's tableland.
A Quaker preacher from Iowa
with two dead babies
and two that lived, she talked softly

to her husband, a godly farmer,
and called the Quaker village
in West Texas their promised land.
They loaded up and left
with nothing but a letter
to lead them. This flat prairie

with waving buffalo grass
reminded them of bread without yeast,
the unleavened body of the Lord.
The only milk here flowed in the cow
roped to their wagon,
their only honey, words in a book.

Caught in a Storm on Hardscrabble

Under an oak, I wait out a hailstorm,
caught in a summer day gone dark,
thunder so loud I can't hear myself

yell to the gelding. I'd rather be
back in the bunkhouse, taking my chances
with poker. Isn't my life worth more

than a gelding so spooked he's stomping?
I grab my Stetson and sling holy water
over the dust. The worst thing to do

is crouch under the only tree around,
a lightning rod. I've tried leading this
stubborn fool into rain, but he won't go,

dumber than steers, which go on grazing
afraid of nothing but hunger. I should
hobble the horse, wade out and hunker down

in my poncho. Grass floats on the plains
like seaweed. Coyotes and rattlers
may slink here two by two, the only shelter.

■ ■ ■ ■ ■ ■ ■ ■ ■ ■   15

At last, the gelding lowers his head
and eats, believing my lie that we're safe,
that nothing can hurt us.

Watching for Ships off
Padre Island

Bring back the days of waves slapping the shore,
gulls hovering over us all day, and sailboats
bobbing in the bay. Here where it rains two times
a year, we watch dry clouds on wide horizons

and pretend they're ours, puff balls that blow away
like smoke. Coronado crossed here out of breath,
his polished armor strapped to a mule, clanking,
his soldiers grumbling, begging aid of the Indians,

begging news of Eldorado, begging for rain.
Even his priest faltered, spitting dry wads
and coughing. Clutching a skull, he declared
God was dead in the desert. These were His bones,

behold the eyes like sockets. Turn back,
or join the Indians: they owned the water.
He howled at night and wet the sand
while sleeping. Coronado watched his eyes,

the wild hair stiff under his cowl.
Coronado called these plains a dead sea
turned to sand. We don't know where he rode.
There are signs on every highway

■ ■ ■ ■ ■ ■ ■ ■ ■ ■ ■

claiming his route crossed here, right here.
Nights, we pretend we go away by writing
French love notes in sand on the night stands.
We think of beaches and promise we'll go back.

What if Coronado didn't stumble home to Mexico
broke, but found all he needed and sailed to Spain?
Let's pretend we're Coronado and his new world wife
lying on the beach, waiting for ships, nothing gained

from exploring but his bride's gold deer-skin
dresses and his priest's surprising self-immersion
in the Gulf, splashing, screaming to white gulls
wheeling and gliding his undying love of God.

■ ■ ■ ■ ■ ■ ■ ■ ■ ■ ■ ■

Between the Moon and Me

They may have needed calves
more than the wolves, time enough
for caution back at the smokehouse
with meat to last the winter.

Grandfather knew what was his, and rode
always with his rifle, ready to die
for his cattle. Living on prairies,
my father said, a man wore the law

in his eyes and guarded his barbed wire
with bullets. I found them
under a board in the cactus, their names
scratched deep with the grain

and simple, fading in the drought
and rains of eighty years. *J. W. McCall
& son, rustlers, 1899*. Deep down,
I found their bones, the skulls

and buckles of their belts
around their backs, coiled like the spines
of rattlers. That night, before I called
the deputy I shot pool with in Dickens,

■ ■ ■ ■ ■ ■ ■ ■ ■

I took that long Winchester down
from the mantel and oiled it, and wound it
over and over in oilcloth, and buried it
under the moon, deep down.

The One That Got Away

In time the bleeding stops.
Puddles of mud go back to sand
and blow away. The buck can't
break it off, can't see

what stung and knocked him down.
Even the arrow he feels
flouncing step by step
won't shake loose from his flank.

He runs with it upstream
like an antler broken in a fight,
the dry creek solid,
flies swarming the blood.

For days he will wander,
avoiding the others,
wondering what to do,
what to do.

Nearing the End of a Century

Let this be clear that we are men of sun
And men of day and never of pointed night.
WALLACE STEVENS

Night of the comet, space without angels,
only our eyes to find whatever light
is there. The stars are rose-ember

over coals already gray. Orion
rises angry in the east.
Night after night he prowls the same

black forest of stars, tracking
the spoor of nothing he remembers.
In zipped twin sleeping bags

before Saigon, we claimed billions of stars
to wish on, perfectly foreign,
the absolute absence of meaning.

We counted myths made up by others
like us, needing to believe in something,
projecting filaments like spiders

spinning tales to turn stark fear
to faith. Somehow we survived that war
and raised our share of children.

Nights, you turn for me to hold you,
although I have no answers.
Our best minds query a comet we'll

never see again for clues. Rockets probe
the one unanswered question, millions
of light years back toward beginning,

before myth. We say whatever is,
we'll accept. But we must know,
we must know something.

Goat Ranching

I could let go and live with the goats
that forage our mesquite and cactus,
browsing on grass, salt blocks

and cardboard boxes that tumble up,
and saunter to the tank to drink.
They've never killed a kid by kindness

or neglect, never had to put their kids'
old dogs to sleep, friends
that drool and quiver and stumble

hobbling to our hands. I've never
seen a goat afraid of trouble. Horny,
they strip the bark off cedar posts

and stand for hours in moonlight,
whetting their horns like sabers
on barbed wires.

■ ■ ■ ■ ■ ■ ■ ■

Nothing to Do but Start Over

Bury the milk, and let the trucks be idle.
Even heating vats can't cure this virus
killing all we own. We feed doomed cows their
last crushed grain and lead them faithful
to slaughter, tossing their Holstein heads,

eyes wide and asking why, it's almost dark
and all of us came home, as always.
It's sleep, not dogs, sick cattle need,
not knowing they're condemned. The health
inspector is home, not watching this.

He knows we'll lead them past the last
still water in the tank, out to the pasture
grazed down and dying. We go, four men
on horses behind them, silent as the dogs
nipping at their hooves, but not barking,

knowing something's wrong. All day,
a Caterpillar tractor dug and snorted,
heaping a mountain we hired, here
on dry plains flat enough to last forever,
never enough rain for runoff. It waits,

■ ■ ■ ■ ■ ■ ■ ■ ■ ■

square and yellow, the concave blade gray
but shiny. Dirt scooped from that deep down
is white caliche, silver in moonlight.
We couldn't do this at noon. The excavated
hole is wide, a coliseum, and slopes

so gently the cows believe it's safe,
and enter, wearing their bells, tolling
step by heavy step, muffled, going down.
We count them, easy to count, they stand
so still in the fresh-dug dirt of a silo,

as if waiting to be milked again.
White eyes and gentle faces give them away.
But something's almost crazed about them,
the way they wait without appeal
under a harvest moon. Only the labored

breath and trembling of one sick cow
keeps ringing her bell, no closer to death
than the others. There's nothing to do
but dismount, rifles already in our hands,
take in our breaths and let them out, and aim.

TWO

Crashes

Real

and

Imagined

Bull

Purple-faced, like old plumbers
standing on their heads to pound
a pointed snake clear through a sewer,
my uncles and father argued
Saturday hours away about anything
that moved, or didn't move.
They never budged, never conceded
the world wasn't flat, the weather
the same, the kids my age wiser
and wilder. Facts like barbed wire
fenced them in, old bulls snorting
at each other. They huffed
and pawed up curses like dirt,
daring each other to find a logical
gate they hadn't tried. My aunts
and mother left them alone
in the den, and weaved their own
pleasant way through pastures
of laughter and gossip, secrets
I believed they whispered about girls
I needed to know, things more urgent
than old stale wars my father
and uncles kept bringing up like cud
and chewing over and over.

■ ■ ■ ■ ■ ■ ■ ■ ■   29

The Eyes in Joe Hall's Shed

The dust in Joe Hall's father's shed
reeked like the air of inner tubes.
Something was there that shouldn't be,
already rotted dry or molded,
hung up on nails on rafters, buried
in boxes, in the jumble of hames of horses
and buzz saws, the dust-gray heads

of moose and deer and wolves. Low
and long like a bunkhouse, that shed
never had lights. Joe stole his
father's keys the summer before it burned
and let us in. He pulled the door
almost shut so no one would know,
and we were alone in the dark,

like a tomb of our own digging.
Whispering, bumping together,
we crept along under the dead eyes
of the moose, the fangs of wolf heads
snapping at pinpoints of light. Swirls
of cobwebs old and dusty sagged over us
like tattered fishing nets strung up to dry.

Staring, I saw them slowly sway,
as a breath from the door passed over,
slow as a ghost moaning at midnight.
Nothing else moved, no spiders,
no scurry of mice. Billy Ray wet his pants,
and lied that he always did, this time
of day. In the dark of Joe Hall's shed,

better to be called baby than coward.
We were used to dust and things
that crawl and scuttle across the floor
at night, and hiss, born poor in the Texas
depression. But here was nothing
we wanted to touch, stale dust
we never smelled outside a funeral home.

I shuddered, and imagined dying,
trapped here for the night.
Whatever was here knew every dim
inch of the room, heard every
breath. The eyes of animals
followed wherever we crept. Once,
when I glanced, they looked away.

My Father Quits Another Job

A hat in his hand and beer on his head,
my father had led his best friend home again,
both stomping their feet and beating snow
from each other's coats. Dried blood like scabs
stuck to his lips, the bridge of his nose.
The other man looked worse.

They fumbled a chair for Mother. My father
turned his hat like the gramophone
he found her once at an auction.
He cleared his throat. The other man,
passing through from somewhere, watched him
with glazed eyes like the prodigal's father

at home. My father had it again—
one guy doing for the other, he announced.
His mustache quivered. That's all
makes this pigsty of a world
worth living in. His grin
could have swallowed the house.

I felt I could fall between his teeth
and disappear. My mother watched her hands.
He tried to reach her hands across the room.
Can't you see, Annabelle, I love
these sonsabitches. I'm gonna quit
that stinking plant and write.

Later, his best friend snoring on the couch,
my father gone to his den,
I left him roaring ballads to my mother,
our thin walls throbbing like the gramophone's
dry membrane coming loose. Outside, wet snow
falling fast covered their tracks.

I shut my eyes against it. I felt it
puff my face like angel kisses
my father gave once with his lashes
when I came home in tears, holding me tight,
like the heavy coat that seemed now, outside,
the only thing between me and freezing.

The Winter They Bombed
Pearl Harbor

The winter they bombed Pearl Harbor,
my brother finally let me follow
up the deepest snow drift in the town.
Each blizzard whipped between two homes

and piled dead-end on Joe Hall's shed,
long and low as a bunkhouse. Drifts
seemed like hills on plains so flat
I'd never seen a sled. In weeks,

my brother was off for war, and he dragged
and carried me up to the roof of the world.
Holding me high by one hand, he dropped me
like a flag up to my crotch in snow so soft

I believed if he let me go I'd sink.
There must have been something else
we did up there, Ed and his friends and me
the tag-along. But even if he let me fall

and had to tunnel down to save me,
if I sank, I can't recall. I've stared
and stared at these four pictures of us
like climbers, but nothing clicks. I'd like

to think I understood where he was going,
what war was and risk, and what
a brother meant. Even now, I try
to feel that afternoon, reach down my feet

on something solid I remember and hold
it all and turn it over like a snowball
in my mind, now that I'm old enough to value
loss, but I can't bring my brother back.

The Guilt of Survivors

Old Uncle Bubba loved hunting owls
better than cards or square dancing.
Most any winter night we'd see him
loading his Plymouth pickup, ready to roll.
Gimp-legged, he had fought at Bataan,
one of the last airlifted out

before it fell. He had scars
I knew made him a hero,
but he hated owls, living alone
since childless Aunt Myrtie died.
Game wardens warned him for years:
shoot squirrels, but leave our owls alone.

But winter came only once a year
like Easter or Memorial Day.
So Uncle Bubba bounced downtown at night
over brick streets wavy with sink holes
like old graves, turned right
at the courthouse with a clang

and clatter of trotlines, cans of worms
and long cane poles bobbing almost
to the bricks. Gone fishin',
the backfire of his pickup bragged,
lurching away from the only red light
in town. One night after the first

deep killing frost, he let me
climb inside the whiskey-smelling cab
and made me hold his long-necked bottle
until the last brick street turned to dirt,
the sway and swerve of rubber tires
crunching over ruts like quail bones.

The trees were spooked behind the bouncing
brights of the pickup, the dirt road
dodging trunks and fences just in time,
weaving through timber like a trail
laid out by drunks. At the river
he slid to a stop on pine needles

under the moon. Whoever was out tonight
liked being alone, the woods so quiet
I could hear Uncle Bubba wheezing,
reaching deep under the pickup dash
for his pistol. He took the bottle
like a hammer and led me down to the water.

■ ■ ■ ■ ■ ■ ■ ■ ■ ■

Gray-white geese on the flyway floated over
in shimmers of moonlight, the river low
for the season. For hours, Uncle Bubba
cuddled that bottle, singing old country
and western and cussing his luck
for outliving my daddy, his only brother,

and Aunt Myrtie and the baby
stillborn in the war, and all those men
on Bataan who didn't survive.
I remember him shaking his head
and singing. I think he said how sorry
he was being alive, and it scared me,

him with a gun and a bottle. That's why
he hated owls, that weren't afraid
to be alone at night, always killing
and being useful to farmers and wardens
and anyone who hated rats, always asking
who he thought he was to keep on living.

  ■ ■ ■ ■ ■ ■ ■ ■ ■

Loading a Shotgun

What enters my hand is red
and hard, like a roll of dimes
capped with brass. I weigh it
in my sweaty palm, up and down,
not heavy, not naked and slick

like a bullet. My father stands
above me, and watches. It enters
the tube of the shotgun, the muzzle
full-choked for impact,
the tightest explosion

toward any target. I close it
and hear it snap. Now it is
loaded, a barrel blue-black
and deadly. Now I can kill
whatever I point at,

like a wand. I listen
with ears tuned tight, and hear
rabbits far off in the pasture,
the soft mourning of doves,
the flutter of wings over water.

■ ■ ■ ■ ■ ■ ■ ■

Flood Fishing

Upriver, the hens keep tumbling in
like lemmings. Fences flooded
by spring rains set them free to peck
worms washed up and sliding
to the river, luring the hens to banks
that crumble like frost.
All night down by the river you can see
white hens float by like chunks of ice.
All night you could cast and cast
and never get a bite. Crappie and bass
are feasting deep on the runoff of worms.

Like love, the only way is to feed them
what they want, dangling your line
along the bottom, the night fog coiling
over the river as if searching for survivors.
The woods are still on such a night.
But sometimes an alligator gar thick as an arm
reaches up and strikes, the white hen
melting from the river before your eyes,
the gar's broad tail splashing
as if the hen were still alive,
flapping to rise up on its wings
and fly, the dark trees on both banks
listening, the thin fog moving on.

■ ■ ■ ■ ■ ■ ■ ■ ■ ■

Crawling through Caverns

Crawling through tunnels, a man keeps his compass
handy. It could be fierce little fish
in a pool, without teeth but vicious,
nipping his wrists and thrashing as if he were
food. Or bats suddenly above him on his knees,

breathing soft breaths, eyes closed
in the glow of his headlamp. Somewhere deep
in the earth he may stumble and rise again,
light blinking out, without landmarks, the polished
stone perfectly innocent of dust, without tracks.

If he crawls two cautious steps
and pauses, marveling at rocks, the whorls
of stone tunnels, like sliding through arteries
or the muscular folds of vaginas, he may not lose
himself until later. It may be pools he has seen

before, stalagmites he has held in his hands
to wiggle past, or the same dripping stalactites
he is sure he lay down and thrust on his back
to squeeze beneath. It may seem like hours,
puzzled that perhaps his watch has stopped

or sprung back when he fell. It may be
the thin totally colorless fish he comes to
in a shallow pool, the fish that does not
shrink from his light, eyeless, the stubborn
carplike lips opening and shutting in silent

absolute darkness. He will lift the compass
to his eyes, to that sole shaft of light
on his skull, and at last find the difference
between the needle's dark and silver points,
the long dark tunnel in, and out into the light.

With a Woman Who Looks Like Crystal Gayle

Listen too long, and you know it.
Your tired ears reach for the sky
like bad guys, enough, enough.
Even your eyes ache after watching
so many sad notes dance by in this
dark smoky bar. Nothing can stop
loud country and western tunes
plugged in and wailing through
speakers tall as coffins.
Belly up to the bar and order
Coors or Bud, and watch them
bring you Lone Star. No matter,
sweet darlin's back at the table
waiting, pulling on empty lips
of a bottle amber as her long
straight-hanging hair. Grab both
long necks in one hand and flick
pale ashes with your thumb,
waltzing slow steps and sliding
down in the calfskin chair
beside her, feeling mean
enough to sit here listening
to fiddles all night long
and yelling sweet words in her ear.

■ ■ ■ ■ ■ ■ ■ ■   43

The Night of Rattlesnake Chili

Only the lure of a rattler kept us
jerking dry tumbleweeds back
from the bunkhouse. Already, cook had
chili boiling, peppers and beef
convincing us all we were starving.

Cursing, throwing empty bean cans
at our horses, cook swore he'd douse
the fire and dump our dinner to the mules
unless we brought him a long dry tail
of rattler. I had heard of cooks

crazy enough to grind rattles
like chili powder, a secret poison
to make a pot boil darker than whiskey.
Kicking and calling each other names,
we scoured the yard for an hour,

a ranch so cursed with snakes
jackrabbits weren't safe while mating.
At last, I grabbed one by the tail,
the writhing muscle trying to escape
down a burrow, and Billy Ray shot it.

Cook cut off the tail and grinned,
held up the ticking rattle, then
crushed and ground it in his hands.
Hulls floated down into red steam,
and simmered. That night, we ate

thick chili redder than fire
and griped about the dust and hulls,
but begged for seconds. Even our beer
was cold and sweeter than most
and steel spoons melted in our mouths.

The Way the World Ends

On a saddled stallion
I was watching the sun
burn itself out
in billowing red clouds,

the plains horizon
flat and long enough
to prove the earth is round.
Behind me, out of the east,

a jet, overhead by the time
I heard the roar,
the contrail like a comet,
the bomber burning white

twelve miles or more
straight up in sunlight,
chasing the sun,
and gaining.

Crosswind Landings

Yaw, and the earth seems bent
on landing, even the wide runway
drawn at odd angles to your eyes
keen on the true track of final.
You should be meeting head-on
fields and turnrows slipping beneath,
but stiff crosswinds won't let you.
Like the rebel you were always
afraid not to be, you crab into the wind
and let the devil take it,
gear down and locked,
airspeed steady enough in gusts,
rented Cessna whining
like a scared fair-weather friend.

Let the black-streaked runway,
your only world, bend steep and savage,
keep your fists loose
on the wheel and throttle,
both boots rammed on the rudders,
hold it off, off against the wind
inches above the concrete,
and at the last second before a stall,
kick the nose cone perfect
and the tires will touch.

■ ■ ■ ■ ■ ■ ■ ■ ■

Crashes Real and Imagined

We have seen them crash
on television, the silver
of thin aluminum plummeting,
trailing dark plumes of smoke
we focus on, the dubbed-in sound
inversely shrill.

Unless it's a newsreel,
planes disappear behind cliffs
or convenient forests,
where waiting crews explode smoke bombs.
Few of us watching films fear death
by impact. We believe

they're dead already,
the blood of bitten capsules
streaming from their mouths,
heads slumped like robots shorted out.
The night Tom Starky died
in pilot training, straight in

  ■ ■ ■ ■ ■ ■ ■ ■ ■

from twenty thousand feet,
we believed his instructor's word
that nothing could force a jet
straight down like that but a coma—
hypoxia, or heart attack.
We knew he risked his own life

trying to save him, diving steep,
screaming on mayday channel *pull out!*
pull out! For weeks
we waked from our private dreams,
feeling our own too solid flesh
impacting in the common ground.

Jet Flight, the Early Years

We'd ease down into cockpits
wired to explode, hook up
and pressure-test pure oxygen
of our other planet. From then on

talk was crisp as sparks,
keyed by gloved thumbs and only
for survival: taxi and takeoff,
climb and maintain two-niner thousand.

Airborne, wheels up and locked,
we swung our eyes like incense on a chain,
blessing our dials and tip tanks,
our wings, in skies that high, bright as armor.

Free of the thrum of propeller blades,
jet loops were smooth implosions,
rolls were clean swirls of the earth
before our eyes. Hardly a flight

went by without hot spots
in our crash helmets, hardly a week
without a jet exploding in midair,
each flight a mission, a quest

for distance, for smooth insertion through mach,
climbs into space delicate as frost
and record dives, wings melting in contrails,
altimeter spinning like a clock gone mad.

None of us could hear the roar we made
sweeping down over canals and bridges,
approaching the airfield swift as night,
slicing the silent throttle back

and pitching steep above the runway,
feeling the spirit of wheels
whir down and lock. And turning final,
falling, advancing the throttle

and only then hearing the chorus of rotors,
flames that caught and sustained us
down to the runway, holding off,
at last cutting the power, the thunder of fire.

We Called It Entering Heaven

You dive there mainly on a dare:
Heaven's Gate, two rocks the size of towers,
straight up from the desert floor.
No rules forbid it, except survival.
Nothing lives there but lizards and ants
scaling sandstone like a Jacob's ladder.
Banked ninety degrees, a jet would fit, we said,
like making love. Grease it with speed.
Nothing under five hundred knots would count.
From twenty thousand feet, split-S,
and level out at five, and glide
head on toward those twin devil's towers
two minutes more, time to think, time
to line up the only perfect approach
you dare. Now, doing the most
insane worship of your life,
you're level, nudging the throttle
to hold five hundred knots,
rolling with aileron and rudder
perpendicular to the only earth
you've known until now,
face to face with two levels
of stone, trying to dive
through the eye of a needle.

■   ■   ■   ■   ■   ■   ■   ■   ■   ■   ■

New Guy

I saw girls squatting against the wall,
and backed out, surely the men's shower,
and it was, the sign said it was mine,
my first day under mortars and rockets

at Tan Son Nhut. Only men lived
in those barracks. Resigned, I entered
the wide corridor of open showers.
They never glanced at me, three girls

and a wrinkled woman. This was their
stall, after so many rooms to scrub,
mops propped in buckets before them
like bamboo stakes. They seemed camped

for the day, with Asian patience.
Two other men scrubbed themselves naked
in suds, and ignored them. With miles of maps
to go over before I slept, facing the wall,

I stripped, shivered and soaped in the cold
water of Saigon, my eyes closed,
listening underwater to alien voices
like angels speaking in tongues.

■ ■ ■ ■ ■ ■ ■ ■ ■ ■   53

War Games

Crouched in a sandbagged bunker,
lights out, listening for rockets,
we played the game with nothing
in our hands, pretending dice

clicked in our fists and hit the dirt floor
rolling. Snake eyes, boxcars,
the point to make, someone
calling our luck, no one

we could see, all of us in this
together. Rockets that crashed down
on the base always killed somebody else.
We played with nothing to lose,

the crews on night shift
risking no more than us,
no sand bunker safe from a hit.
We rolled till our luck ran out,

passed the empty handful
to the next man kneeling
in the dark, bunkered down,
having the time of our lives.

■ ■ ■ ■ ■ ■ ■ ■ ■

We never knew the color of scrip
we lost, not caring
what was at stake in night games,
not daring to think.

When the all-clear siren wailed
we lifted our winnings from dust
and left through the reeking tunnel
into moonlight naked as day

and climbed the steps of our barracks
to wire springs tight as our nerves,
lying in rooms flashing red
from flames in the distance.

Christmas Bells, Saigon

Buses came late, each driver sullen,
head shaved above the ears. At the French
country club on base we nursed warm drinks
while French and their Viet Cong cousins
ignored us, strolling from room to room.

The maître d' said wait, he'd find a place
for us. For hours, we stumbled around outside
trying to get drunk. After weeks of rockets
we needed to celebrate. Someone joked
the clerk who took our reservation

died in last night's rockets. People I knew
kept disappearing. I asked what's going on.
Vietnamese friends all looked at me
and shrugged. Men who'd been in Vietnam
for years kept dancing off with girls.

I listened for gunfire above the band's
loud brassy mix of Beatles and Japanese.
I studied guards buried in cages
ten feet above us in trees. Five minutes apart
they rattled bells to signal —what?—

We are alive? How could anyone believe
in bells dangled on barbed wires?
Sappers smart enough to count
could slit the guards and keep it up,
ring-ring, till all guard stations fell.

Two sergeants and I sat on a verandah
and wondered where all the girls had gone,
when a bus to the barracks would come,
blamed bad French planters for the war.
Even with rockets, I wanted to lie down

and dream of peace, rumors of good will
toward men. We agreed on all things true
and noble, sober on gin and French vermouth,
listening to Japanese Beatles and the bells,
the bells all through the night.

THREE

For

Friends

Missing

in

Action

Rig-Sitting

On the derrick, I twist this wrench tight
as if the oil pipes of the world depended
on it. I clear myself and signal,
and down below, the clang
and rattle of chains begins,
the drill bit biting miles through bedrock.
Now it goes on without me, nothing to do
but watch the black shaft turning.

Hardscrabble cactus grows a quarter
of an inch each decade. All afternoon,
mesas pretending to be mountains
bump into clouds from another county.
The only rain all month was rumor.
Like waterbugs, antelopes in the distance
wade the mirages. Living on air,

hawks ride out the drought, dipping
and staring. I sit up here and wonder
how many times they can circle,
how many angels dance in a whirlwind,
how many times a bit goes around
before breaking.

Cousin Billy and the Weather

Spinning his wheelchair, he'd rise up
suddenly for air and fall back,
yelling old-fashioned gospel songs
to keep him human. No one loved noise

like Cousin Billy, deaf and crippled
in the war. He kept radios blasting
in all rooms, on different stations,
a battle of empty decibels. I turned them

down so I could hear, but found them
twisted loud when I came back
with liniment and magazines, items
he scribbled on a list. He kept pistols

on each window ledge, sat up some nights
alone in moonlight, the best hunter I knew
before the war. He shot coyotes from his room,
and rattlers, wild turkeys and skunks

fool enough to waddle close. At dawn
he wheeled outside and cleaned whatever
he could eat, jerking the wheels in ruts.
He hated rain, sticking in mud and falling,

singing *Help,* yelling *On Jordan's*
Stormy Banks I Stand, cursing and crying.
I'd find him outside, or naked in the tub
scrubbing blood from the chair, his shoulders

bulging. I lined up dates with girls he knew,
nothing but songs and bullets on his mind
after the noise of Saigon, cursing
game shows on TV, radar and weather charts

all he would watch, shoving inside the room
to see the maps, the rise and fall
of the jet stream, the stalled squall lines,
the highs and lows of regions under siege.

After the Noise of Saigon

If where we hunt defines us,
then stalking this steep hillside
dark with spruce makes sense,

more than the dreams I've floundered in
for years, trying to fathom signs
all night and wading ashore

disgusted. Switches dripping sap
keep flipping me when I glance
over my shoulder for spoor

I might have missed. Evergreen
needles sting when I swing my head
face-forward for clues. Isn't this

the strangest nightmare of all,
knowing my aim with a bow
is no better at twenty yards

than forty? But here I am, alone
with a cougar I've stalked for hours,
climbing until I'm dizzy.

These blue trees have nothing
and all to do with what I'm here for
after the noise of Saigon,

the simple bitter sap that rises in me
like bad blood I need to spill
out here alone in the silence

of deep woods, far from people I know
who see me as a friend, not some damned
madman stumbling for his life.

For Friends Missing in Action

Into this tunnel of dirt
deposit quick thoughts
of a corpse
like savings. Pitiful beer

can't dig him up
from seventy shovels of earth,
but toast him over and over.
Here lies a flier

missing since Saigon
fell in the seventies,
sixes or sevens
if he cratered deep in a swamp,

brought down in flames
from twenty thousand feet
by a rocket, or languished,
chained to a bamboo cesspool.

He's gone.
Lift up your savage mugs
and let the truth ring
like a gong: he's gone.

An Object Set in Motion

Pilots believe bad crashes
   come in threes. Not simply
      engines that flame-out

or overheat, dead-sticked
   to fire trucks waiting
      by runways. Not even

midair collisions of planes
   in formation, if both
      limp home and touch down safe

without stalling. Death
   alone makes faith in fate
      and tarot cards seem simply

the way it works. If nothing
   happens for days after one
      crash, it's over. But if two

go down a mile or oceans
   apart, watch out.
      Wheels are in motion.

■ ■ ■ ■ ■ ■ ■

As children, we held hands
in a circle, squeezing
and giggling, while someone

outside our magic circle,
the one we called *it*, walked
slowly around us, faster,

the flying dutchman
beginning to smile to himself,
then running. All of us squirmed,

hardly breathing.
We dreaded being *it*,
feared the stunning touch

of his hand, the signal
to run, to run for our lives
though he was halfway around

and no one ever made it
back to clasp hands
safe in a circle of friends.

Fathers and Sons

My son does not fear death by drowning.
At twelve, rafting the Brazos,
he tried white water alone
and spilled. Grasping,
he grabbed sheet iron or glass.

It slashed his right hand
to the bone. An Austin surgeon
spliced tendons, arteries.
But the nerves, like thousands
of coaxial cables.

I row behind him now,
bass at Buchanan impossible to find
without live bait and luck.
He waits more patiently than I
for nibbles like ghost code

on the rod. Nights in a bass boat
we row deep water
like two who went blind together
tangling each other's lines
with fingers learning to feel.

Breathe Deeply, and Relax

There's always something to be done
alone. Even a group plan
pays only eighty percent
of reasonable charges.

The rest is yours,
the deductible off the top,
whatever unreasonable fees
the surgeon charges.

When you were young, sometimes
at night you prayed you'd never
have to be alone again,
but you were,

always, even when your mother
held you while a corpsman
stitched your leg, ripped
in the tree you fell from.

Even the first time your husband
helped you breathe
while you endured
and naturally delivered.

Even tonight, when you lie down
with a houseful of children
finally asleep,
safe in your husband's arms,

close enough to dreams
to recognize their ensemble voices
drawing you a few more hours
to themselves.

Night Missions

Tonight will be like any other night.
At two or three the phone will ring
soon as I've drawn the first good hand.
I'll spread the cards face-up,
knowing solitaire won't peek. Pecos,
Abilene, it could be anywhere
south of Denver, someone badly burned,
skull crushed like a hardboiled egg,
needing a surgeon in the southwest
who could put him together again.

I fire up number one, then two, propellers
spinning so smooth the Cessna shudders
until I release the brakes. I taxi out,
in the red glow of the cockpit
I run the checklist, flip on collision lights
and find all gauges in the green.
I hit the runway, firewall both throttles
and line up on the roll.
Banking, I'll clip the moonlight,
blue wings climbing somebody's dreams,
tuned blades humming like mercy.

■ ■ ■ ■ ■ ■ ■ ■ ■ ■

Backpacking the San Juan

On a blue spruce mountain
across a mile of meadow,
a flash of light
in the treeline—field glasses,
or gunfire.

I lift my glasses.
A thousand one,
a thousand two. A deer
darts through a clearing

and sound whines past me
like a bullet. Suddenly
I'm a mile away
crashing through branches,
each bounding leap my last.

The Middle Years

Now it begins, the soft insinuation
of ferns through spark light. The final
campfire flame is gone, unless we breathe
on embers. Shadows of piñons flare up

and fall away like ghosts. You whisper,
Will these coals live? Nothing
that breathes risks even this much light,
to be seen by strangers deep in the forest.

For hours we gave ourselves
to simple tasks, unfolding, the clang
of steel on steel stakes for the tent,
finding sticks to build one fire for water

that boils without getting hot. This high
in the mountains, air is scarce as friends.
Close on a common stone, we watch rose embers
wink like mountain lions. The last sparks

fling away from this spinning planet
and burn up in the only air there is.
All those years to make a roof for children,
gone from us faster than sparks.

Now we are back to beginnings
deep in the mountains, one fire at a time.
Stars are our comfort, and ferns that sough
and hover over us all through the night.

We lie in eiderdown and hold each other
a long time, silent. Later, I wake
and listen. The quick cry of a coyote
rises in the distance, the sound

of wings lifting, eagle or owl.
Nothing else for minutes, only your
steady breathing, asleep, believing
nothing's out there that shouldn't be.

Balance

This far out in the country
   pronghorns the size of fawns
    tremble and stare,

dip down and graze
   as they have done forever.
    This range grows nothing but pale

yellow yucca and cactus and grass
   like dried moss, almost green.
    Hawks living on thermals glide

in a summer sky so blank they wheel
   without cover of clouds for hours,
    waiting for rabbits or mice

to dart into sunlight. Lower,
   slower, another is slithering,
    flicking his tongue at the sun,

testing the hollow desert wind,
   the wind like a god,
    the wind always delivering.

■ ■ ■ ■ ■ ■ ■ ■

The Children's Hour

Let's try spinning autumn into gold.
If straw spun for Rumpelstiltskin,
leaves already bronze may blaze.
Our rakes go back, go back under shrubs,
over roots, combing the lawn like yarn.

The neighbors' mockingbird
twitters and clucks in the sweetgum,
flashing its tail and teasing.
Pile after pile, we heap up leaves,
wishing the wind would wait,

chasing them with our rakes
like loose coins rolling toward the curb.
Late afternoon, yard combed,
rakes put away, three shiny black bags
bulge with money, if time is money.

We heave them into the dumpster,
hiding our hoard with others' trash.
Years back, we raked loose leaves
and let our children splash, tossing leaves
like money, then called them to help rebuild

a castle of leaves, and touched a match.
Flames the color of gold leaped up
and changed dry leaves to fire
brighter than the sun going down,
all of us shielding our eyes and silent.

Sundown

He's not alone, the old bull
hump-shouldered by the barn.
Scars like braided whips on his back
pucker in the cold, like other bulls

backing off. He snorts,
and flicks his tail.
Night coming on,
he has walked stiff-legged

and swaying to his stall,
no longer tossing his horns,
no longer expecting one of his herd
to be there waiting, her narrow back

and barrel turned toward him,
quivering. Always a trough of grain
is there in the shade,
and he goes for it now without desire,

without fighting the pain in his nose,
the ring long a part of him
like the cramp in his legs
he takes with him everywhere.

Eyes glazed, he lowers his head
and eats, blowing the dust,
the hulls. Finished with all that
at last, he waits

on four legs in the dark
and listens to his farm, the last hens
clucking, the snort of horses
in the barn, the faint

swishing of cows' tails,
and somewhere far off
a dog's persistent barking.
He closes his eyes,

leans a degree for balance
and feels the barn,
the weight of the farm
and the long day disappear.

Old Men Fishing at Brownwood

Spitting tobacco juice on hooks,
we skewer silver minnows that writhe
in the light of the moon, lining our boat
with bass fighting for all the line

they're worth. These are the shallows,
the home of the moccasins, deep mud
of the turtles. Our flat boat wallows,
bumps over stumps, and stalls. Slowly,

slapping mosquitoes, we pole it off
and glide in moonlight between branches
like scarecrows. What we desire
winnows the dark under logs

flooded for years, in tunnels of reeds,
deep pools in the shallows. We believe
we will know what we need when we find it,
though it may take nights on still water,

for we are too old to turn back, to settle
for perch in the daylight, willing to risk
pneumonia or stroke, the hiss of fangs
nearby on a shimmer of water.

Between Two Shores of Toledo

Swimming Toledo Bend last summer,
we were afraid of nothing but boats
with drunk drivers. Miles out from shore,
we felt like hitchhikers, motorboats
like Porches stopping to offer rides.

Waving, treading water, we watched them
glance at each other and roar away,
the wake of their Mercury motors
bobbing, swamping us in the troughs
between two shores of Toledo.

At last, far out on the lake,
we rolled and rested on our backs.
The sun was white fire
blurred between blinks squeezed open.
I remember waves at eye level,

your fingers nibbling my own
like fish. We floated alone
between shores miles apart, thousands
of miles from our children at the ocean.
I heard it close in my ears, the roar,

the constant roar. Without a word,
with a nudge a wave might have made,
we rolled and went on swimming,
knowing we'd passed the point of no return
on a lake swarming with skiers.

Tiring, we reached through waves
that always looked the same,
as if we were going nowhere.
We fought the urge to thumb down boats
and let them drag us aboard. Giddy,

glimpsing each other swallowing air,
we kept on crawling through water
for a shore we believed was worth it,
no matter how many more skied by
holding by one hand and laughing.

Reasons for Taking Risks

I could have died when I was ten
in the Brazos, diving blind
in water red as the bank.

I might die old, after long silence,
the sad way we say of fathers,
at last he's at peace.

I could have died climbing the Oberon
last summer, trying hard to release
my son's looped rope.

Pitons and karabiners
like the tightest bonds
break loose. But it was dark

when we reached the summit.
We stood a long time staring
as if the night would never end.

The Rodeo Fool

We hummed sad country songs all summer,
certain the bulls we shoved were worth it.
Nothing thrills a family crowd more
than a cowboy falling, even the king
of the cowboys, and one or two hurt bad
each night. They know riding bulls is brave
and crazy. They like a good stomping,
when rodeo clowns help them die laughing
in the face of danger, a black
two-thousand-pound bull pawing dirt,

goring the cowboy over and over. They scream
so loud they can't hear the screams
of the cowboy. I run out waving my arms
like an angel in makeup and baggy pants,
slam into the bull's broad butt,
grab his tail and twist and twist. The bull
stops goring and lifts his horns.
I'm wiping my hands up and down my pants
hung by suspenders up to my nipples,
like rubber waders Baptist preachers wear.
The bull looks back, stupid on all four
massive legs. The crowd loves it,

safe in the stands, munching beer nuts
and guzzling. I twist the tail till it burns,
drop it and wipe my hands three times
and make a face, then fake a double-take
at the bull's black eyes deciding
by god to kill me. I run,
hoping my aim for the rubber barrel
is better than it was two years ago.
By now, Jay or Billy Ray has dragged
the rider to safety and runs out
baiting the bull. The bull snorts,
swinging his head between us, tail limp,
testicles drooping like a water balloon.

The fool's baggy pants and derby
are a good costume to hide the blood
if the bull's tail-wise and quick
to gore anyone messing with his butt.
No one at rodeos pays to see clowns suffer,
clowns make it fun to watch a grown man
gored and stomped on by a beast. It can't be
bad as it seems if a fool in baggy pants
can shove a bull and crank his tail
and live. Even when we're gored,
bleeding inside our baggy pants,
ribs crushed, unable to breathe,

we pull ourselves up and double over,
bowing. We go on making believe it's fun
all the way from the arena:
it's in the rules. I couldn't say how many
stitches and crushed ribs, how many bones
Jay and Billy Ray and I have broken
and grown back. They couldn't pay me
enough to do this, if friends didn't grin
and raise a hand when we lift them
into the ambulance. People leaving

laugh at me and wave as if I'm some kind
of saint, a fool holy enough to do what
they'd like to do, nightly to save someone
from death and make believe it's fun.
My stupid moves prove nothing wild
is as wise and dangerous as men.
Because of me, they ride home humming,
not troubled by tons of metal hurtling
past their bumpers, believing death's a black bull
mad and charging, all men are brave and cunning,
that all fall down, get gored and trampled on,
all men are able to rise with the help
of clowns, able to look death in the eye,
to wear a clown's face, laughing, and walk again.

THE
JUNIPER
PRIZE

This volume is the thirteenth recipient
of the Juniper Prize
presented annually by the
University of Massachusetts Press
for a volume of original poetry.
The prize is named in honor of
Robert Francis (1901–87),
who lived for many years at
Fort Juniper, Amherst, Massachusetts.